INSIGHTS

ANCIENT EGYPTIANS

FIONA MACDONALD

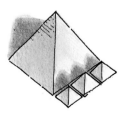

INSIGHTS

ANCIENT EGYPTIANS

FIONA MACDONALD

BARRON'S

Library of Congress Catalog Card No. 93-16415

International Standard Book No. 0-8120-6378-3

Library of Congress Cataloging-in-Publication Data

Macdonald, Fiona.
   Ancient Egyptians / Fiona Macdonald. — 1st ed. for the U.S. and Canada.
   p.   cm. — (Insights)
   Includes index.
   Summary: Illustrations and text provide information about life
in ancient Egypt, covering the pharaohs, family life, the Nile River,
arts and crafts, temples and tombs, and more.
   ISBN 0-8120-6378-3
   1. Egypt—Civilization—To 332 B.C.—Juvenile literature.
[1. Egypt—Civilization—To 332 B.C.   2. Egypt—History—To 332 B.C.]
I. Title.   II. Series: Insights (Barron's Educational Series, Inc.)
DT61.M23   1993
932'.01—dc20   93-16415
                                                                              CIP
                                                                               AC

This book was designed and produced by Quarto Publishing plc
The Old Brewery, 6 Blundell Street, London N7 9BH

Consultant Henrietta McCall
Art Director Nick Buzzard
Senior Editor Kate Scarborough
Designer Doug Whitworth
Illustrators Sharon Smith, Jim Robins
Picture Researcher Louise Edgeworth

The Publishers would like to thank the following for their help in the
preparation of this book: Karen Ball, Trish Going

Picture Acknowledgments Key: a = above, b = below, l = left, r = right, c = center

Quarto would like to thank the following for providing photographs and for
permission to reproduce copyright material. While every effort has been made
to trace and acknowledge all copyright holders, we would like to apologize
should any omissions have been made.

Ashmolean Museum, Oxford, pages 10ar, 25ac, 37bl, 42ar; Cairo Museum, pages 18ar, 26ac, 29ar;
Peter Clayton, pages 11cr, 15cr, 17bl, 23bl, 31b, 34ar, 34br, 39br, 47ar, 50ar, 50bl, 51al, 51b;
James Morris, pages 11ar, 12ar, 12bc, 14br, 15al, 15ar, 16br, 17br, 20b, 21al, 23al, 23br, 23ar, 28br,
30al, 30b, 35ar, 38cl, 38b, 38r, 39ar, 39b, 40br, 41br, 42bl, 43ar, 43bl, 43cl, 46al, 46b, 47bl, 47br, 49ar;
Andrew Stewart, pages 11al, 13bl, 13br, 13ar, 17ar, 18cr, 19br, 20ar, 24ar, 25bl, 26al, 26bc, 26b, 27al, 27c, 27bl,
27br, 28ar, 34bl, 35al, 37al, 40bl, 44bl, 46ar, 48br, 49bl, 49br; Times Newspapers, page 45a; UNESCO/Nena Dovic, page 12bl.

Front jacket photographs supplied by: Ashmolean Museum, Oxford—above,
left, James Morris—above center & left, Andrew Stewart—below.
Back jacket photograph supplied by: Andrew Stewart.

Manufactured in Hong Kong by Regent Publishing Services Ltd
Printed in Singapore by Star Standard Industries (Pte) Ltd

3456   9620   987654321

CONTENTS

WHO WERE THE EGYPTIANS?

The ancient Egyptian civilization lasted for many centuries, from around 3000–300 BC. During that time, the Egyptians created massive buildings and elegant works of art. They invented systems of writing, measuring, and counting. They developed a strong, centralized government, served by well-trained scribes and officials. Egyptian designs, and technological achievements, were admired—and sometimes copied—in many countries of the ancient world. And their mysterious, complicated religious beliefs still fascinate scholars and writers today.

The earliest Egyptians were nomads, wandering in search of food and water. But by around 2900 BC, at the time of the first recorded Egyptian ruling family, they had been settled in villages along the banks of the Nile River, for hundreds, perhaps thousands, of years.

From these simple beginnings, the Egyptian state grew very strong. Egyptian kings, known as

▲ Earliest Egyptian?
A portrait of a bearded man from the earliest-known period of Egyptian civilization, before 3050 BC. This statue is made from black basalt, a hard, shiny stone.

▼ Rich builders
The rulers of Egypt were enormously wealthy. They used this wealth to build magnificent temples and tombs. This map shows a few examples of the monuments they created.

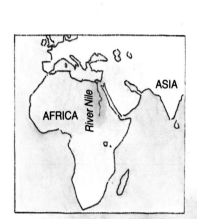

▲ Egypt in Africa
The kingdom of ancient Egypt grew up along the banks of the Nile River in North Africa. It was well positioned for contact with both Mediterranean and Middle East early civilizations.

▶ A fertile land
The Nile River provided a long strip of fertile land, ideal for growing crops. Including the delta, it covered about 13,000 square miles (34,000 sq km). The ancient Egyptians settled on its banks around 3000 BC and formed one of the most sophisticated early civilizations.

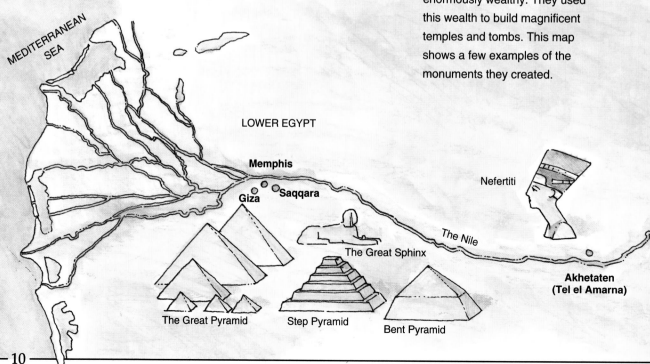

MEDITERRANEAN SEA

LOWER EGYPT

Memphis

Giza Saqqara

The Great Pyramid

Step Pyramid

Bent Pyramid

The Great Sphinx

The Nile

Nefertiti

Akhetaten
(Tel el Amarna)

◀ Khufu's pyramid

The pyramid of Pharaoh Khufu, at Giza, in northern Egypt. Often called the Great Pyramid because of its size—it is 486 feet (146 m) high and covers 2,556 square feet (230 sq m). Pharaoh Khufu ruled between 2551–2528 BC.

▶ Well-known evidence

One of the most famous objects to survive from ancient Egypt. The gold burial mask made to cover the face of the mummified Pharaoh Tutankhamen, who died around 1323 BC.

pharaohs, ruled a large empire. They fought and conquered far-away peoples, in present-day Syria, Libya, and Iraq. They traded with merchants from other ancient civilizations, such as the Lebanese and Greeks, who lived around the Mediterranean Sea.

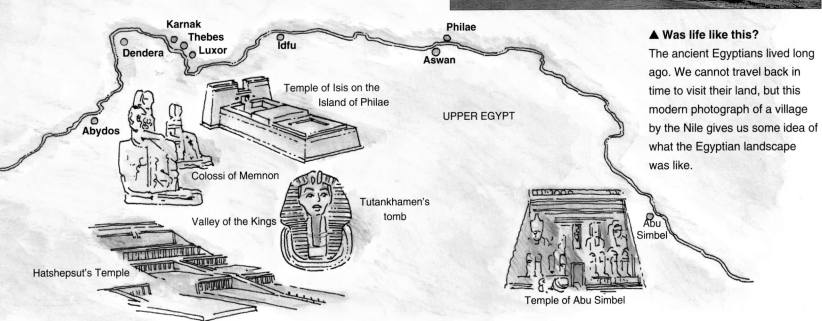

Karnak
Thebes
Dendera Luxor
Idfu
Philae
Aswan

Temple of Isis on the Island of Philae

UPPER EGYPT

Abydos

Colossi of Memnon

Valley of the Kings

Tutankhamen's tomb

Hatshepsut's Temple

Abu Simbel

Temple of Abu Simbel

▲ Was life like this?

The ancient Egyptians lived long ago. We cannot travel back in time to visit their land, but this modern photograph of a village by the Nile gives us some idea of what the Egyptian landscape was like.

How do we know?

Even though the ancient Egyptian people lived so long ago, we can still find out about their life-styles, customs, and beliefs. Our information comes from different kinds of evidence—buildings, statues, tombs, inscriptions, and many smaller objects—that have survived from ancient times.

Evidence from art

Thanks to Egypt's warm, dry, desert climate, many monuments have survived remarkably well. These tombs and temples were decorated

▲ Valuable evidence
A wall-painting from the tomb of Sennedjem, who lived around 1300 BC. It shows him, with his wife Iyneferti, busily occupied after death. Above them, the hawk-headed god Horus holds the "ankh," a symbol of everlasting life. Paintings like this tell us about Egyptian crops and farming techniques, as well as about Egyptian religious beliefs.

MOVING MONUMENTS

Pharaoh Ramses II (1290–1224 BC) built the temple at Abu Simbel. It is guarded by four huge statues of Ramses himself. Twice a year, rays from the sun shone inside the temple, and lit up statues of gods, carved in the rock.

In 1964, a new dam was planned at Aswan, to bring water to lands nearby. It would raise the water level, and the temple would be flooded. The United Nations launched a rescue operation. The whole temple was cut out of the cliff face, piece by piece, and moved to a new site high above the river.

▲ Moving the face of one of the huge statues of the pharaoh.

▶ The rebuilt temple entrance at Abu Simbel.

▶ Attracting visitors
Tourists have been fascinated by Egyptian remains for thousands of years. These modern tourists are visiting the ruins of the great temples at Karnak, near Thebes.

RE-CREATING THE PAST

Egyptologists—people who study the ancient civilization of Egypt—use many skills to help them understand the past. By learning about Egyptian art, architecture, paintings, carvings, and inscriptions, and by digging up or excavating ruins, they are able to "re-create" the past, in words and pictures.

▲ Archaeologists digging up the past in Egypt.

▼ **Ancient ruins**
Many of the buildings created by the ancient Egyptians are now ruins. But using imagination…

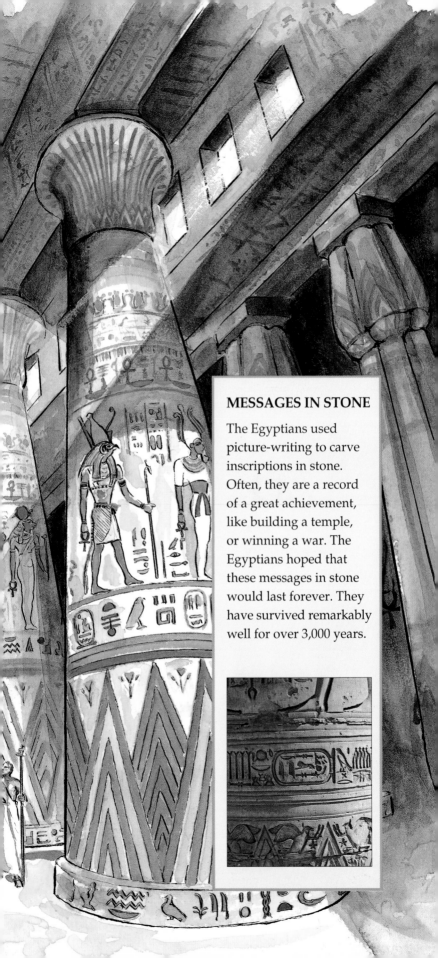

MESSAGES IN STONE

The Egyptians used picture-writing to carve inscriptions in stone. Often, they are a record of a great achievement, like building a temple, or winning a war. The Egyptians hoped that these messages in stone would last forever. They have survived remarkably well for over 3,000 years.

with carvings, paintings, and statues. Some show everyday activities, other show religious scenes. They all tell us something about the way the people lived—how they fought and farmed, went hunting, said their prayers, or simply enjoyed themselves. They also help us to discover what the Egyptians looked like, what they ate, and what clothes they wore.

Writing and carving

Most Egyptian buildings, and many works of art, are decorated with inscriptions—lines of picture writing called hieroglyphs carved into their hard stone surface (see pages 18–19). Because stone is so tough, and lasts so long, these inscriptions can still be read even after many centuries have passed. We can also learn about the Egyptians from travelers, such as the Greek writer Herodotus, who visited the country around 500 BC. These travel-writings are often very useful, but we cannot believe everything they say.

▶ **A forest of columns**
...we can make good guesses at what palaces and temples looked like. They were built with magnificent "hypostyle halls"—rooms where the roofs were supported by carved and decorated columns. Often, they were painted to look like reeds.

PHARAOHS AND PEOPLE

To the Egyptians, their pharaoh was more than just a king; he was the living image of a god, come down to earth. As such, he was respected, feared, and occasionally, worshiped. The pharaoh was the only person who could speak directly to the gods in their temples. He gave them gifts of food and wine and, in return, asked them to send blessings to the people he ruled.

▼ A social pyramid
Egyptian society was arranged rather like a pyramid. The pharaoh was at the top. Then came high priests and nobles. Lower down were priests, officials, and army commanders The fourth layer included skilled craftsmen. At the bottom came laborers and peasants.

As well as having religious duties, an Egyptian pharaoh was responsible for running the government. He had to maintain law and order, protect temples, and lead his armies to war.

A pharaoh also had to be good at managing people. He needed to win the support of powerful nobles and chief priests, to stop them plotting against him. He had to make sure that his

pharaoh

nobles

officials

▶ Mighty pharaoh
This colossal stone statue of Ramses II stands outside the temple that he built at Luxor.

craftsmen

laborers

◀ In the living rock
Statues carved in the rock face at the tomb of Quar, at Giza, not far from the Great Pyramid. Many officials and priests were buried here, to be near the pharaohs.

▼ A royal sign
The bezel (decorated center) of Pharaoh Akhenaton's silver ring. It shows his name in hieroglyphs.

government officials used their power to benefit the country, not just to make money for themselves. He received foreign ambassadors in his palace, and made peace treaties with kings and princes from distant lands. Often, this meant marrying a foreign princess, to strengthen the alliance. Some pharaohs had a great many "official" wives.

RELIGIOUS REFORMER

Pharaoh Akhenaton ruled from 1353–1335 BC. He tried to introduce a new religion, based on the worship of just one god—the "Sun Disk." But this new religion was banned after his death.

CROWNED IN GLORY

Pharaohs, and sometimes gods, were portrayed wearing several different types of crown. Each crown had a special meaning. And on ceremonial occasions, pharaohs also wore a false beard, made of tightly plaited hair, ornamented with gold and jewels.

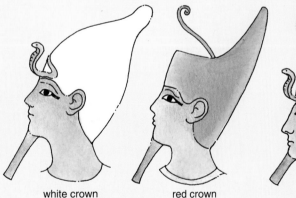

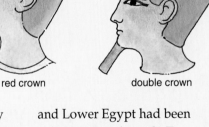

white crown   red crown   double crown   war crown

The white crown was traditionally worn by kings of Upper Egypt—the lands in the southern part of the country. The red crown was traditionally worn by kings

of Lower Egypt, the marshy northern lands around the Nile delta. Ever since Pharaoh Menes, who came to power around 2920 BC, the two kingdoms of Upper

and Lower Egypt had been ruled by one pharaoh. To make this clear, many pharaohs chose to be portrayed wearing a double crown, that is, the red and

white crowns together. A smaller, blue, war crown was worn whenever the pharaoh led troops into battle.

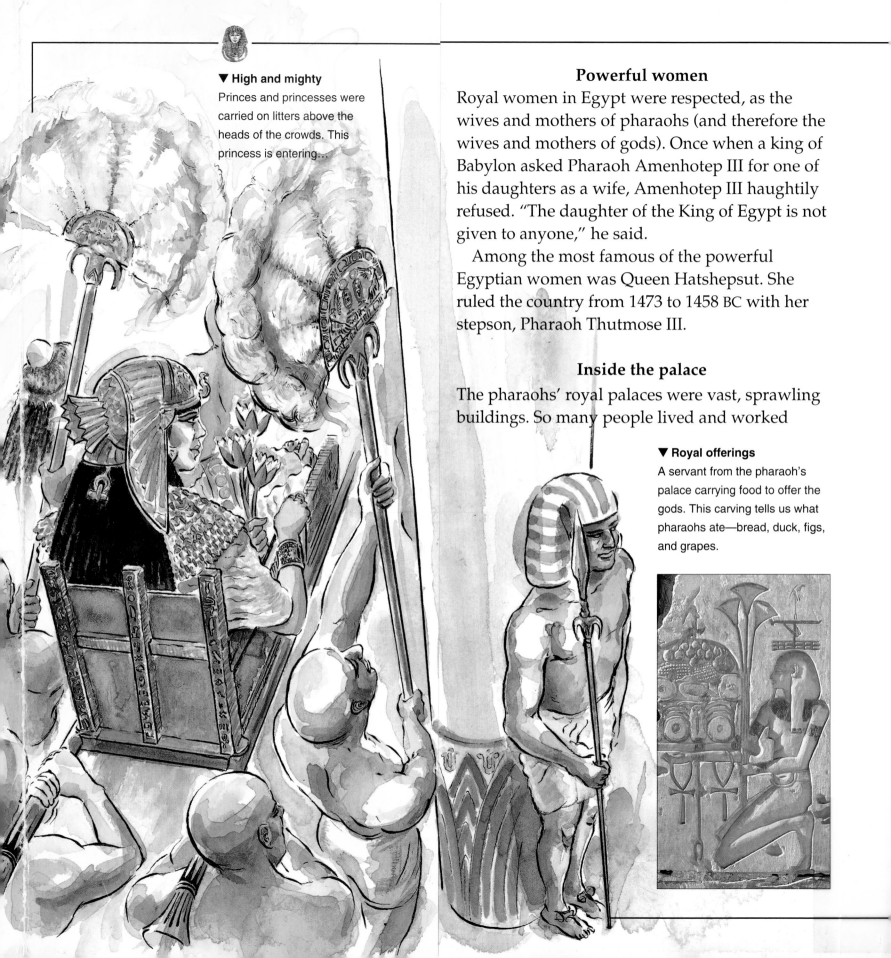

▼ High and mighty

Princes and princesses were carried on litters above the heads of the crowds. This princess is entering…

Powerful women

Royal women in Egypt were respected, as the wives and mothers of pharaohs (and therefore the wives and mothers of gods). Once when a king of Babylon asked Pharaoh Amenhotep III for one of his daughters as a wife, Amenhotep III haughtily refused. "The daughter of the King of Egypt is not given to anyone," he said.

Among the most famous of the powerful Egyptian women was Queen Hatshepsut. She ruled the country from 1473 to 1458 BC with her stepson, Pharaoh Thutmose III.

Inside the palace

The pharaohs' royal palaces were vast, sprawling buildings. So many people lived and worked

▼ Royal offerings

A servant from the pharaoh's palace carrying food to offer the gods. This carving tells us what pharaohs ate—bread, duck, figs, and grapes.

there that they were more like little villages than family homes. There was a great reception hall, where the pharaoh received royal visitors, listened to his advisers, and granted—or refused—requests from petitioners groveling on their knees. There were private rooms and bedrooms for the pharaoh and his family, offices for his ministers, and guardrooms and quarters for soldiers and servants.

Comfort and luxury

Egyptian palaces were built of dried mud bricks. But life inside was elegant, comfortable, and luxurious. Royal palaces could be two or three stories tall. Hollow channels between the floors allowed cool breezes to circulate, a simple form of air-conditioning. By the time of the New Kingdom, many places had lavatories and even showers. After a shower, pharaohs and their families would retreat to the nearby "oiling room," where their skins would be massaged and softened by smooth, scented oils.

▲ Relaxing at home
This carving shows Pharaoh Akhenaton with his wife Nefertiti and their daughters. Akhenaton's palace was furnished with many rich and beautiful objects, made of wood, pottery, gold, and glass.

DANCING GIRLS

Pharaohs and their courtiers were entertained at feasts in the palace by dancers and musicians. Favorite instruments included harps, drums, and cymbals. Egyptian dancers were well trained and acrobatic. Tomb paintings show dancers performing cartwheels, somersaults, high-kicks, and even the splits. Other entertainers included wrestlers and storytellers.

BUREAUCRACY

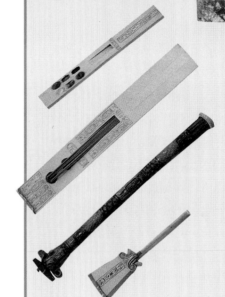

The geography of Egypt makes it a difficult place to rule. It is a very long country, about 750 miles (1200 km) from north to south. Apart from a narrow, muddy strip along both sides of the river—and even this is sometimes flooded—the land is desert. In ancient times, there were hardly any roads. The best way to travel was along the river, but this was very slow. It could take about three weeks to reach Nubia from the city of Memphis. How could the pharaohs keep control?

Successful pharaohs coped with this problem of government in two different ways. They relied on trustworthy local governors (chosen from among noble families or top officials) to rule the provinces for them, and they recruited an enormous number of scribes. The scribes, along with certain other officials, sent and received royal messages, and kept detailed records of everything that concerned government, law, and taxes. Many of these records have survived. They can tell us a

RECORDING TRIBUTES

Scribes (above) also kept records of tribute payments. Tribute—paid in food, treasures, or by sending men to work—was collected by the pharaoh's officials from ordinary people.

◀ From top to bottom: palette for mixing ink; scraper for making corrections; pens made of reed; pen case.

MAKING PAPYRUS

The tall papyrus reeds were chopped into short lengths and then peeled. The inner pith was sliced into thin strips.

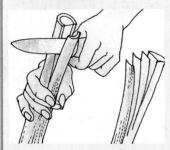

The strips were arranged in layers on a wooden board. They overlapped in a crisscross pattern.

They were then covered with a cloth and pounded with a heavy mallet. This made them stick together into a single sheet.

The cloth was removed and the newly made sheet of papyrus was polished with a smooth stone. It could then be trimmed.

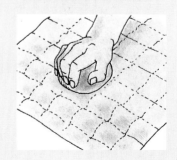

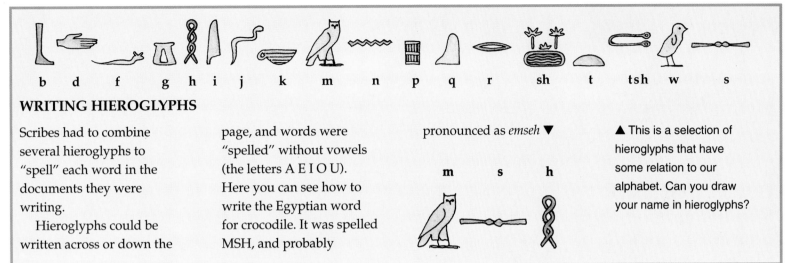

b	d	f	g	h	i	j	k	m	n	p	q	r	sh	t	tsh	w	s

WRITING HIEROGLYPHS

Scribes had to combine several hieroglyphs to "spell" each word in the documents they were writing.

Hieroglyphs could be written across or down the page, and words were "spelled" without vowels (the letters A E I O U). Here you can see how to write the Egyptian word for crocodile. It was spelled MSH, and probably pronounced as *emseh* ▼

m   s   h

▲ This is a selection of hieroglyphs that have some relation to our alphabet. Can you draw your name in hieroglyphs?

lot about how the Egyptian government worked.

It took a long, slow training to become a scribe. Trainees started young—before they were 12—and were made to work very hard while learning. Sometimes they were beaten—the Egyptians had a saying, "a boy's book is on his back."

Picture writing

Egyptian scribes wrote on paper called papyrus that was made from reeds. They used ink made of soot. Sometimes they decorated their writings with red ink, as well. The Egyptians were among the earliest people in the world to invent writing, in around 3000 BC. They wrote using picture symbols, known as *hieroglyphs*. Some hieroglyphs stood for the sounds that make up words, others stood for ideas, or for actual objects. For example, the hieroglyph for the sound we make when we say "r" was an open mouth. The hieroglyph for the idea of drunkenness was a jar of beer.

▶ **Book of the Dead**

Egyptian scribes wrote many books, which have been preserved in the dry desert air. This pages comes from a *Book of the Dead*. The picture shows a king (on the far right) making offerings to the gods. The writing describes how funeral ceremonies should be performed, and what each stage in the ceremony means. Books like these provide valuable evidence about Egyptian hopes, fears, and religious beliefs.

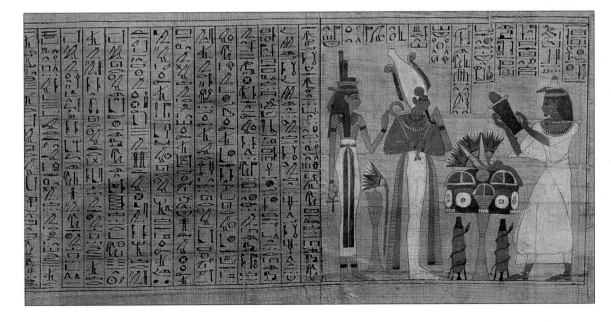

PHARAOHS AND EMPIRES

The Egyptian government was well prepared for fighting. The pharaohs maintained a standing army, lodged in barracks in important cities. These troops were tough, well fed, and fit.

The first main period of expansion came during the Middle Kingdom when Egyptian troops occupied Nubia. It was a land rich in treasures—gold, ebony, ivory, leopard skins, and black African recruits. Later, during the New Kingdom, the Egyptians attacked the civilizations of Syria and Palestine. Again, they went in search of loot.

Around 1640 BC, Egypt was invaded by a group of people from foreign lands called the Hyksos, who stayed for over 100 years. A further series of attacks came around 1190 BC, from groups of warriors based in countries to the north and west. The Egyptians called them the "peoples of the sea," and eventually defeated them. As Pharaoh Ramses III proudly reported, his ships defended the coast "like a strong wall." Egyptian warships, which were driven by oars as well as sails, were faster and easier to steer than enemy craft.

Bloody battles

Warfare was brutal. Ramses III also boasted that he had seen his enemies "overthrown in their blood, and made into heaps." Pharaohs, wearing a special crown, led their armies into battle surrounded by handpicked troops. The early Egyptians fought with bows and arrows, spears, clubs, and axes. Chariots, curved swords, and body armor were introduced later on. After the time of the Hyksos invasion, Egyptian craftsmen

▶ **War leader?**
This wall-painting shows a pharaoh wielding a battle-ax, clutching captives. Pictures like this can be misleading. Not all pharaohs went to war, although many were portrayed fighting.

▶ **Frontiers of empire**
The lands ruled by Egypt, and the frontier areas where pharaohs fought with peoples living nearby.

Hittites
Greeks
Sea peoples
MEDITERRANEAN SEA
Assyrians
Canaanites Babylonians
Libyans
Persians
Nile River
RED SEA
☐ Egypt 20th Dynasty
☐ 21st, 22nd Dynasties
Nubians

◀ **Miserable tribute**
A slave sent as tribute from Nubia, conquered by the Egyptians.

▲ Warriors in wigs
A painted wall-carving showing Egyptian soldiers ready for battle, armed with shields and spears.

▼ Battle chariot
A pharaoh rides into battle in his light, fast chariot. Usually, a chariot was manned by two soldiers, a driver and an archer armed with arrows and spears.

copied designs for deadly, high-powered bows from their Asian neighbors. Most soldiers carried shields, did not wear helmets, and fought barefoot. Both sides in a battle fought to kill. But if any of Egypt's enemies were captured alive, the men were forced to fight in the Egyptian army, or were sent to work as slaves.

WEAPONS OF WAR

Egyptian soldiers fought mostly on foot. They aimed to scatter the enemy by a sudden, fierce attack. Weapons included spears for throwing, long and short swords for slicing, ax-heads, stone-tipped arrows, and heavy wooden clubs.

club head

spear head

ax

ax-head

arrow head

sword

sword

arrow head

HOUSES AND HOMES

We know that Egyptian builders had the skills and technology to construct large, elaborate homes. But most Egyptians did not have the money to pay for these palaces. So where did the vast majority of ordinary people live?

We can get some idea of what ordinary houses were like in ancient Egypt by looking at model houses that have been found buried in tombs. We can also look at surviving Egyptian houses built in the traditional way. Both were constructed of sun-dried mud, covered over with a thin layer of plaster. Both were built to a simple, squarish design, with a flat roof, sometimes topped by a terrace where the inhabitants could sit and enjoy the cool, fresh, evening air. Inside, the rooms were small and dark, with narrow windows (sometimes covered with cloth) and low ceilings. Some houses had two stories, others were all on one level. Many had cellars for storage, dug into the rough ground underneath.

Most people lived in villages, clustered along the banks of the river. Village houses were built close together, for strength and security. The villages were surrounded by ditches and fields. Nearby, was the bleak, inhospitable, endless expanse of the desert—for the Egyptians, "the home of the dead." At certain times of the year,

BUILDING BRICKS

Egyptian bricks were made from Nile mud, mixed with water and finely chopped straw (1).

This sticky mass was stirred well, then packed carefully into square or oblong wooden molds, smoothed down, and left in the hot sun to dry (2).

As the water evaporated, each brick became solid. Then the bricks were turned out of their molds to allow the drying to finish (3). When ready, the bricks were rock hard, and very strong. Finally, they were carted, a few at a time, to the building site (4).

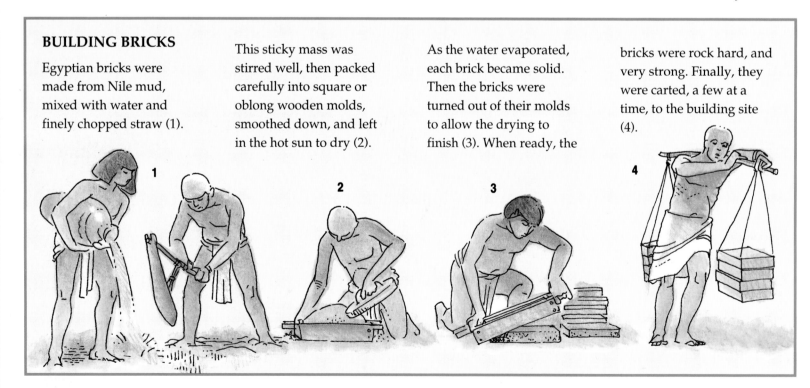

THE OLD AND THE NEW

The Egyptians invented many important construction methods, which are still used today. The left-hand photo shows mud-brick arches in storerooms built at Thebes about 3,100 years ago. The photo on the right shows a modern building near Luxor, which uses very similar techniques.

particularly in springtime, hot desert winds blew dust and sand into every corner of Egyptian homes.

Birds and beasts

Various forms of wildlife also found their way into Egyptian houses through cracks in the plaster, or between crumbling bricks. Some, such as swallows and house martins, were harmless; others, such as rats, flies, and mosquitoes, spread dangerous disease. People feared snakes and scorpions most of all; their bites were painful, and could kill.

◄ **A link with the past**
Making mud bricks in Egypt today. The mud is mixed, shaped, and dried.

▼ **Traditional homes**
In the countryside, many Egyptian people still live in mud-brick homes like these.

FAMILY LIFE

Today, most of us can expect to live until we are about 70 years old. This was not the case of ancient Egyptians. Then, life expectancy was short: on average, people lived for 20 years. This suggests that many people died very young, some lived to perhaps 30 or 40, and a few lived longer. We have no precise figures, but it is likely that many, if not most, babies died before they reached their fifth birthday. Only the strongest survived.

These figures had an effect on family life. People got married much younger. For example, Tutankhamen married when he was only ten. The Egyptians must also have gotten used to the frequent death of babies and toddlers.

For many Egyptians, especially women, family life was important because their house was also their place of work. Indoors, women and their older daughters cooked, cleaned, and cared for young children. They used the courtyards of their homes for grinding corn, drying fish, plucking waterfowl, baking bread, and brewing beer. They might also spin thread and weave rough fabric for the family's clothes. During busy seasons, they

▼ **Women's work**
Egyptian women made most of the clothes for their families to wear. It was skilled, time-consuming work. These two women are weaving cloth from flax. Most Egyptian cloth was plain, but Egypt became famous for its fine linens.

◀ A devoted family
Tomb model of Seneb and his family around 2200 BC. Seneb was a chief valet and royal tutor.

▶ Daily bread
This tomb model shows a woman grinding corn. Women were in charge of all the food preparation in ordinary homes. They helped to weed crops, feed animals, and gather in the harvest, as well.

▼ Work at home
The woman at the back is washing flax and pulling it into strands. The threads held by the woman in the front have been spun and are ready to be woven into cloth.

would also help their husbands and brothers who were out working in the fields.

Food and drink
The Egyptians had fifteen different words for bread. For almost everybody, it was the most important item in their diet. It was made from

◀ The world's oldest basket?
This basket, over 4,000 years old, was woven from reeds and grass.

BEER FROM BREAD?

This model, found in a tomb, shows a popular subject—brewing beer. The brewer is bending over a large pottery vat, stirring crumbs of part-baked bread into river water. Often this process was done by men standing inside the vat, trampling the bread and water with their feet. After mixing, the liquid was left to stand in the sun until it fermented. Then it was strained and stored in clean jars. Most household tasks were performed by women but, from the evidence of models and carvings, brewing seems to have been a male specialty.

▲ Fetching and carrying
Wealthy Egyptians had many servants, both men and women. This graceful wooden statue shows a woman servant carrying a heavy box, probably containing food offerings to give to the gods. It was made around 2020 BC.

an early form of wheat, called emmer wheat, coarsely ground between millstones or in a hand-held *quern*. Egyptian bread was made without yeast, so it was flat and quickly became stale. It may have looked like the pita bread we buy today.

A simple diet

Other staple foods included beans, onions, and dried meat. The fertile soil around the Nile provided a large amount of fresh fruit and vegetables, such as leeks, cucumbers, radishes, dates, nuts, and melons. Wild birds like geese and duck were caught and eaten. Many people also ate fish. To drink, there was river water, beer, or wine for the rich. Beer was probably safer than plain water, since the alcohol it contained acted as a mild disinfectant. It was made from old bread mixed with plenty of water and stored in covered

▶ Multipurpose
Oil was used for cooking, in cosmetics, and for lighting. This pottery lamp burned olive oil.

▶ Knife-edged
This knife, used to prepare food, was made of flint. Its edge is surprisingly sharp.

jars in the sunshine until it fermented. It must have looked like a very muddy soup. Most people liked to strain it before drinking. Many pottery beer-strainers have been found.

Feasts and festivals

Food was important in religious festivals and seasonal celebrations. Paintings in tombs show pharaohs and wealthy families feasting on roast duck, beef, honey cakes, fruits, and wine. Not everyone could afford this level of luxury. At a feast, diners were waited on by servants, and entertained by musicians, acrobats, and dancing girls. Women sometimes sat separately from the men. To complete the festive mood, the women carried sweet-smelling lotus blossoms, or else wore cones of perfumed grease, which slowly melted in their hair.

▲ Storage jar
Jars like this were used to store oil, wine, beer, or water. They were made from local clay by skilled Egyptian potters.

UNWELCOME GUESTS
Rats, mice, and insects brought diseases into Egyptian homes. From the evidence of mummies, Egyptians seemed to have suffered from several unpleasant conditions—from diarrhea and worms to sores and blindness—all caught from animals.

▶ Pots—but no pans
Metal was precious in ancient Egypt. Bowls and pots for cooking were therefore made of clay.

◀ Dinner is served
Egyptians ate from plates made of pottery, sometimes decorated with trailing clay patterns.

▲ Beer strainer
This basket sieve was used to strain things like beer, which could not be drunk before straining because it was so gritty!

THE NILE RIVER

Without the Nile, Egypt would not exist. There would be no water, and no fertile land to grow food. Egyptian rainfall is low, about four to six inches (100–150 mm) in an average year. The climate is hot. Even in winter, temperatures seldom fall below 55°F (13°C). The surrounding desert lands show the natural results of weather conditions like these.

But Egypt has the Nile. It is one of the world's greatest rivers and flows for a vast distance— about 4,160 miles (6,690 km)—in a valley bordered by rocky cliffs and hills. Once a year, between July and October, the Nile flooded, and covered the valley floor with a thick layer of mud and silt. Over many centuries, this had built up into a layer of damp, warm, rich soil. It is where the ancient Egyptians lived and grew their crops. If, as occasionally happened, the Nile floods failed, there was famine in the land. Since the Aswan Dam was completed in 1968, the Nile no longer floods.

A living from the land

Egyptian farmers planted grains, lentils, beans, and vegetables in the wet Nile mud. Crops grew quickly, and gave good yields. The fresh silt every year acted as a natural fertilizer. The farmers dug irrigation ditches to spread the floodwaters as far as possible and to maintain a steady water supply once the flood season was over. They built ingenious machines, such as the *shadoof*, to raise water from the river and pour it over the fields.

Ferries and cargo boats steered a careful course through the winding river channels. Cows, donkeys, rats, dogs, and small children paddled in the waters at the river's edge. Women gathered

▼ Sailing down the Nile
This modern photograph shows boats on the Nile River. Travel by boat is still the easiest way to reach much of the country, as it was in ancient Egyptian times. In this photo, you can see the narrow strip of fertile soil close beside the river, where the land is watered by the Nile floods. In the distance, you can see the dry desert and mountains.

CREATURES OF THE NILE

The Nile River was home to a great variety of animal life, from tiny water snails to massive crocodiles. Most were harmless, but a few were dangerous to people using the river. Mummies have been found with bones that seem to have been bitten off by crocodile teeth. This statue of a hippopotamus found in a tomb dates from around 2000 BC. It looks charming, but, when attacked or frightened, hippos could be fierce.

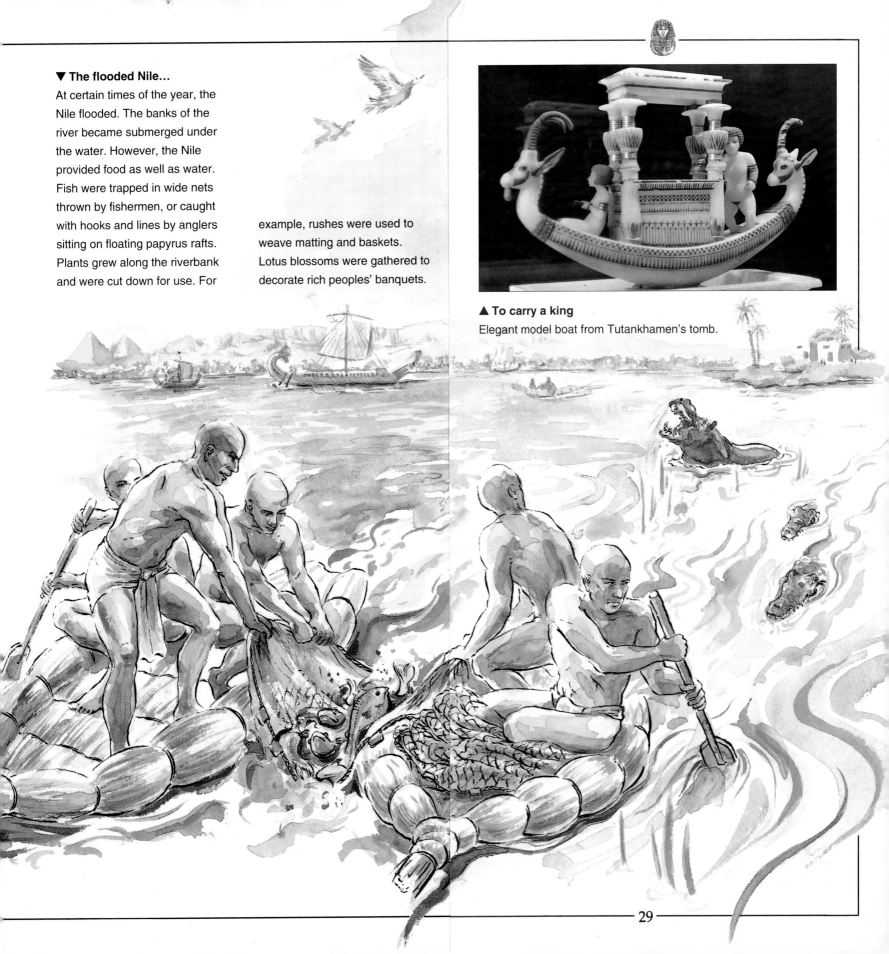

▼ The flooded Nile…

At certain times of the year, the Nile flooded. The banks of the river became submerged under the water. However, the Nile provided food as well as water. Fish were trapped in wide nets thrown by fishermen, or caught with hooks and lines by anglers sitting on floating papyrus rafts. Plants grew along the riverbank and were cut down for use. For example, rushes were used to weave matting and baskets. Lotus blossoms were gathered to decorate rich peoples' banquets.

▲ To carry a king

Elegant model boat from Tutankhamen's tomb.

PLOWING AND REAPING

Plowing and sowing took place at the same time. The plowman drove cattle and plow and the sower walked behind him scattering seed. At the time of harvest, crops were cut down using sickles.

Top: A wooden plow.
Center: A hand-held digging stick, used to prepare the ground for sowing crops.
Bottom: A wooden sickle, with flint teeth.

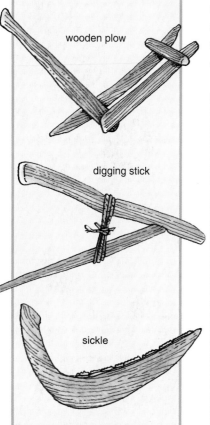

wooden plow

digging stick

sickle

◄ Prize animal
This splendid ox was carved on the wall of the temple of Ramses II at Abydos. It came from the temple's own farms, and had been specially bred and fattened up. Now, in peak condition, it is shown taking part in a festival procession, on its way to be slaughtered as an offering to the gods.

to wash dirty clothes, chatting and laughing together. Drinking water was drawn straight from sewage-polluted shallows. The "river of life" was also a breeding ground for disease.

Hard work

Egyptian farmers probably made and mended many of their own agricultural tools. These were often very simple, and were constructed of wood.

▼ The whip hand
This tomb-painting shows Sennedjem plowing with a pair of oxen. He is driving them forward with a double whip. His wife walks beside him. Egyptian women often helped in the fields.

The tools did the job well if the man (or sometimes woman) using them knew what he was doing and worked hard. There was no time to waste.

As well as laboring in the fields, Egyptian villagers gathered clover and other wild plants to feed their cattle, and cut rushes to make baskets and mats. They reared ducks and geese. They spun wool to make thread, and grew flax in muddy pools. Both were used to weave cloth. Where there was enough land, they planted orchards and vineyards, and harvested apples, grapes, and figs. They used the Nile mud to make bricks to build and repair their homes.

Hunting and fishing

Villagers went hunting for wildfowl in the marshes, and speared fish from boats, or trapped them in nets. Sometimes they went out to kill crocodiles or, less frequently, a hippopotamus. They regarded both as very dangerous creatures. It was also important to try to exterminate the pests that threatened their crops. Mice and locusts were particularly destructive. The Egyptians kept (and sometimes worshiped) cats; a few, belonging to noble sportsmen, were even trained to retrieve birds that were killed with sticks. Cats killed the mice, but nothing could defend the fields from a swarm of hungry locusts. If they arrived before harvest time, then, as one Egyptian poet wrote, "the rich look worried, and every man is seen to be carrying his weapons." Making sure of a good harvest was a matter of life and death.

▲ Hooking a fish?
This stone wall-carving from a very early tomb at Saqqara shows fishermen on the Nile. Notice one of the men rescuing a lamb from the water and from the jaws of a crocodile who looks on from below.

◀ A day's sport
Hunting wildfowl in the marshes along the banks of the Nile River. Wealthy Egyptians enjoyed pleasant days like this in the damp, shady reed-beds, away from the heat and sand, and dust of cities and palaces.

TOWNS AND TRADE

Egyptian towns and cities served two main purposes: they were centers of government and centers of trade. Egypt was divided, for government and taxation, into forty-two districts known as *nomes*. There was a leading town in each nome. In addition, certain major cities, such as Memphis and Thebes, acted as national capitals throughout Egyptian history. The pharaohs built splendid palaces at both Memphis and Thebes.

Many cities were also the home of a god, or, according to Egyptian religious beliefs, were regularly visited by one. The Egyptians believed in many local gods, "the spirits of the place," who often took the form of typical local animals. For example, the hawk-headed god, Horus, was particularly sacred to the inhabitants of Heliopolis. Other cities housed the shrines of major, national gods. At Thebes, there was a magnificent group of temples dedicated to the god Amon. In the desert that lies beyond the opposite riverbank, there were many royal tombs. Pharaoh Akhenaton built a whole new capital, "the City of the Sun Disk," at a site now known as Tel el Amarna, not far from Thebes. But his religious reforms were rejected after his death, and the beautiful city was abandoned and left to ruin.

▲ **Traveling**
Not everyone in ancient Egypt lived in a town or city. Many farmers had to travel to reach trading places. Using donkeys allowed farmers to carry heavy loads to...

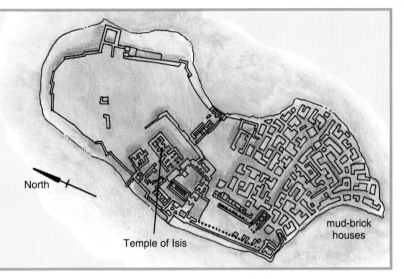

North

Temple of Isis

mud-brick houses

▼ International trade

Goods on sale in Egypt came from Africa, the Middle East, and the Mediterranean world. Trading journeys were long and dangerous. It could take months to bring a precious cargo home.

Merchants from many lands

Memphis, in particular, was a great center of trade. It lay along the bank of the Nile River, which led northward toward the Mediterranean Sea. Merchants from many lands—Syria, Palestine, Libya, Phoenicia, Cyprus, and Sicily—came to its busy harbor and traded and settled there, creating an international business community. Egyptian traders purchased copper, incense, and semiprecious stones, such as turquoise and lapis lazuli, timber for building temples and ships, and fine-quality cedarwood. In return, they exported corn, lentils, papyrus, and linen. Because there was no common currency, or money, international merchants would have exchanged or bartered with different goods or produce.

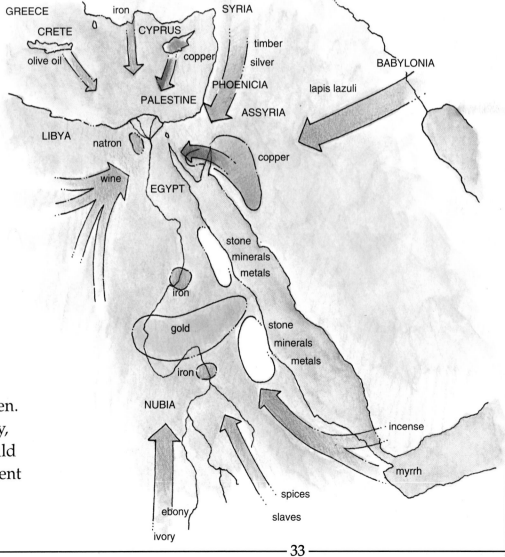

GREECE
iron
SYRIA
CRETE
CYPRUS
olive oil
copper
timber
silver
BABYLONIA
PHOENICIA
lapis lazuli
PALESTINE
ASSYRIA
LIBYA
natron
copper
wine
EGYPT
stone
minerals
metals
iron
gold
stone
minerals
metals
iron
incense
NUBIA
myrrh
spices
ebony
slaves
ivory

ARTS AND CRAFTS

▲ **Glass luxuries**
Glass scent bottle in the shape of a fish. Discovered at Pharaoh Akhenaton's new city of Tel el Amarna, abandoned about 1335 BC.

Egyptian craftsmen were extremely skilled. Like Egyptian farmers, they achieved great success using very simple tools. The materials they worked with were not easy to manipulate. Even so, they managed to produce a high level of finish on carvings, statues, jewelry, and other decorative objects.

In most periods of Egyptian history, artists and craftsmen were content to copy, or slightly improve upon, earlier styles. They followed well-established traditions, which showed respect for pharaohs and the gods. Change for its own sake was not particularly valued; many people preferred something familiar to something new. But, slowly, innovations did take place. Statues of famous people were carved in new poses, and painters began to depict animals, gods, and people in experimental styles.

In Memphis and Thebes, there were many busy craftsmen, all specialists in a particular trade.

Paintings from Theban tombs portray a wide variety of crafts. There were leatherworkers, sandalmakers, stonecarvers, metalworkers, chariotmakers, sculptors, carpenters, jewelers, scribes, and boat builders in one Sixth Dynasty (around 2200 BC) tomb alone. Many of these craftsmen would have worked mainly for pharaohs

▲ **Fragile survivors**
These delicate Egyptian glass vases were made around 350 BC. Glass was made from melted sand, mixed with mineral salts found in the desert.

METALWORKING

Some of the finest Egyptian statues were made of bronze, like the model below of the sacred bull, Apis, who was worshiped in the city of Memphis.

Several steps were involved in making a metal statue. First, a mold was made, usually of clay. This was a hollowed-out block, divided into two halves. Each half showed all the details that would appear on the surface of the finished statue. When the mold was ready, the two halves were joined together, using more clay. Then the ready-mixed metal (bronze is a mixture of copper and tin) was melted over a hot fire. Very carefully it was poured into the mold; the smallest splashes could

◀ **Gilded box**
This box in the shape of a double seal is an example of Egyptian craftwork. Made of gold-plated wood inlaid with glass-paste, it was found in the tomb of Tutankhamen.

▶ **Craftsmen at work**
Painting from the tomb of the noble Rekhmire. It shows potters, carpenters, and goldsmiths.

...nerchant families. But,
...goods to spare, villagers
...o exchange their
...these finely made objects.
...markets and occasional
...d with the Nile flood
...a favorite local god.

...trimmed and polished. A new work of art was complete. Skillful workmen could use the same mold over again, to make more copies of the same statue. But, for large pieces, this was not often done. The amount of metal needed to make a solid statue was very expensive. And not many pharaohs wanted their image to be mass-produced!

carrying the melted bronze

pouring bronze into the hollowed-out mold

trimming and polishing the cast

CLOTHES AND JEWELS

Egyptian clothing was lightweight and very simple. The climate was hot, and the fields and roads were dirty, so young children often went naked. Even so, the evidence of the paintings, statues, and jewelry that have been found in tombs suggests that some Egyptians, at least, were very interested in their own appearance—and in how other people looked, too.

◀ **Everyday clothes**

The servants and laborers wore extremely simple clothes made from rough cloth. Men would wear just a loincloth and women basic shift dresses. Children ran around naked with shaved heads to keep them safe from lice and dust.

For everyday wear, men wore a length of cloth wrapped around their waist—rather like a Scottish kilt. Women wore a long skirt or a sleeveless shift. This could be topped by a loose overdress or a square of cloth tied rather like a shawl. Ordinary people's clothes were usually white, the natural color of linen or wool. Dyes to produce the bright golds and yellows seen in some tomb-paintings were too expensive for most people to afford.

Dressing up

The wealthy, powerful groups in Egyptian society had more money to spend on making themselves look stylish. Their clothes were similar in style to those worn by ordinary people, but made of better fabric. Sometimes it was so fine that it became semitransparent. In some paintings, the loose, flowing robes worn by men and women seem to be delicately pleated. People kept their best clothes for special occasions. One ancient Egyptian poem encouraged party-goers to "put myrrh (perfume) on your head, and clothe yourself in fine linen." Women also wore elaborate party makeup—black eyeliner and green eyeshadow have been found in tombs, along with mirrors, curlers, tweezers, ointments, and combs.

THE LATEST STYLES

Egyptian paintings reveal many different hair-dressing styles. Children and slaves sometimes had their heads shaved, to keep them free from dust and lice. Royalty sometimes grew just one lock of hair long, and wore it plaited over one ear. This was a sign of their noble birth. Adults often wore wigs.

▲ This statue shows a woman wearing a short wig.

▼ Party makeup

Left: an ivory case that contained *kohl*, a black eyeliner used by Egyptian women. Right: a make-up palette for mixing eye shadow colors.

▼ Royal finery

Pharaohs and their wives enjoyed wearing splendid clothes, jewels, wigs, scent, and makeup. Their finery reminded ordinary people of their majesty and power.

GODS AND GODDESSES

I n ancient Egypt, as in many other civilizations, religion, politics, local tradition, and everyday customs were mingled together. It is hard to discover in detail what people really believed. Evidence, such as a few prayers and early texts written on papyrus, tells us that the Egyptians worshiped many gods. It also suggests that people at all levels of Egyptian society, from priests to peasants, were prepared to spend time and money on their religious beliefs. Pharaohs paid for elaborate tombs and temples; peasants gave food offerings, or purchased lucky charms.

Why did the Egyptians have so many gods? Each one served a particular need. Some gods originated in ancient tribal traditions, such as the sacred bull, Apis, who was worshiped, or the cats dedicated to the goddess Bastet. Others, such as the sun-god Ra, developed out of Egyptians' reverence for nature. Some gods were honored throughout the land, some only locally. Some gods and goddesses had special functions. Pregnant women prayed to the goddess Taweret to keep them safe in

▲ God of the sky
This statue of the sky-god Horus, shown with the head of a hawk, comes from the temple at Idfu.

▶ Symbol of eternity
This scarab (dung beetle) represented "eternal life" to the ancient Egyptians. Model scarabs are found in many tombs.

childbirth. Farmers prayed to the gods of the Nile for floods to water their crops.

Justice and good order

Some gods looked human, others had the heads of animals and birds. Many were shown carrying symbols of their powers. In some centuries, certain gods were popular, while others were almost ignored. But one important religious belief hardly changed. This was the idea of *ma'at*: justice and good order. The Egyptians believed that the gods ruled the world, and it was people's duty to live according to their will and to maintain *ma'at*, so far as was possible. For different groups in society, *ma'at* meant different things—soldiers had to fight bravely, peasants had to work hard, and pharaohs had to rule well. Then the gods would be pleased.

CROCODILE GOD

Amenhotep III (who ruled from 1391–1351 BC) with his divine protector, the crocodile-headed god Sobek. Traditionally, Sobek had been worshiped in the marshy lake area known as the Faiyum—probably because many crocodiles lived there, and local people feared them. But gradually his cult spread throughout Egypt. Amenhotep gave generously to build temples, especially at Luxor. This statue comes from the great temple there.

◀ **Fierce lioness**
Sekhmet was the goddess of war. She caused death in battle. This statue comes from the temple of Ptah at Luxor. Ptah was a creator-god, and was often worshiped alongside Sekhmet, the destroyer.

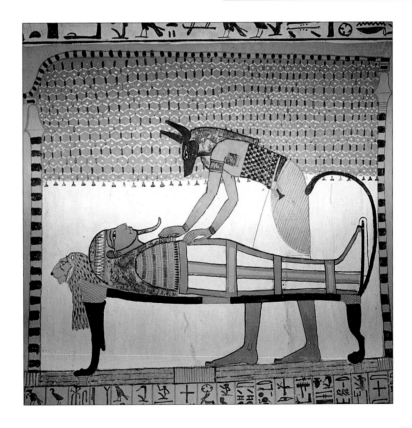

▶ **A guide for souls**
In this tomb-painting, made around 1300 BC, the dog-headed god Anubis is shown bending over a mummified body. Anubis was believed to act as a guide to souls during their journey through the kingdom of the dead.

▼ **Proud and beautiful**
Statue wearing an emblem of the cat-goddess Bastet. She gave life and fertility. Killing cats was forbidden in Egypt.

TEMPLES AND TOMBS

"**B**ehold, the heart of his majesty was satisfied with making a very great monument..." This inscription on Pharaoh Amenhotep III's temple at Luxor explains why these magnificent buildings were built. The "very great monument" showed the pharaoh's power. It showed religious devotion and revealed good taste. Most important, as a monument to the pharaoh and his gods, a temple would last forever.

▶ **Priests and pharaohs**
Pharaohs were religious leaders, as well as being heads of government and leaders in war. They took part in important ceremonies, especially on festival days. Then, the statue of the god was carried in procession through the temple courtyards to the sanctuary, escorted by priests, nobles, and the pharaoh himself.

Most Egyptian temples were arranged like palaces, because a holy statue of the god "lived" or visited there. Every day the statue was in residence, the senior priests washed and fed it. They gave it offerings of food and perfumes. Sometimes, the statue was taken from one temple and moved to another, or was carried in procession through the streets or in boats along the Nile. The Egyptians did not worship the statue itself. Rather, it reminded them of the presence of the god, whose invisible spirit might come to them at any time.

Not all temples were palaces for the gods. Some were built over royal tombs, to worship the memory of a dead pharaoh, and to glorify his achievements in this life. Queen Hatshepsut arranged for a beautiful mortuary temple to commemorate her time in power. It contains almost 200 statues portraying episodes during her reign.

◀ **The cult center**
The temple at Karnak where the god, Amon, was worshiped became the biggest and richest in Egypt. Several pharaohs gave money to rebuild it, including Ramses II, who ruled from 1290–1224 BC. These great statues of him guard the entrance to the temple.

▶ **Built for a queen**
This impressive mortuary temple was built on the orders of Queen Hatshepsut, around 1450 BC, as her memorial. It is carved partly out of the solid rock face, and was originally surrounded by gardens, trees, and statues. It is decorated with carvings showing scenes from Queen Hatshepsut's eventful life.

THE PEACEFUL LAKE

The sacred lake at Dendera, west of the temple of Hathor. Because temples were designed as homes for the gods, they included many features usually found in royal palaces. Lakes were admired for their peaceful beauty—a foretaste of life after death, perhaps? They also provided a cool, pleasant place where priests and worshipers could rest.

THE PYRAMIDS

The Great Pyramid at Giza, made as a tomb for Pharaoh Khufu, is the largest stone monument ever built on earth. Construction work started almost 4,600 years ago. It contains over two million carefully shaped blocks, each weighing, on average, around two and a half tons. All pyramids were made using only the simplest technology without iron tools, powered engines, or wheels. Together, they are an astonishing engineering achievement.

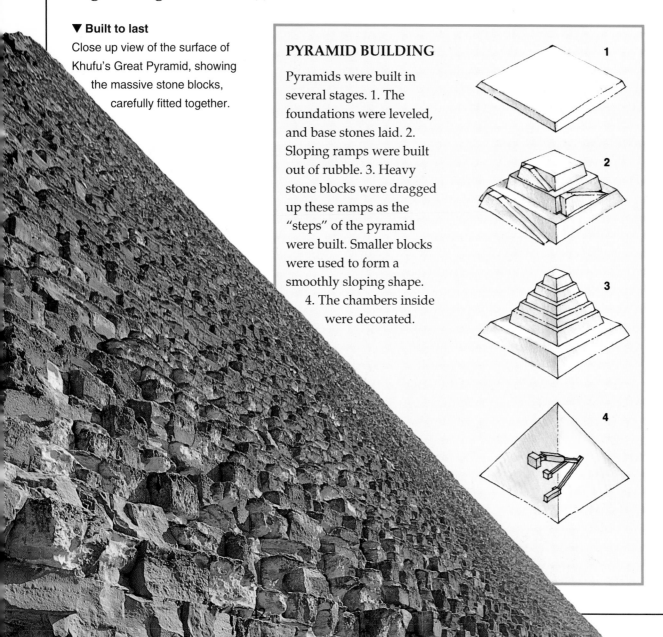

▼ Built to last

Close up view of the surface of Khufu's Great Pyramid, showing the massive stone blocks, carefully fitted together.

PYRAMID BUILDING

Pyramids were built in several stages. 1. The foundations were leveled, and base stones laid. 2. Sloping ramps were built out of rubble. 3. Heavy stone blocks were dragged up these ramps as the "steps" of the pyramid were built. Smaller blocks were used to form a smoothly sloping shape. 4. The chambers inside were decorated.

▲ The architect as god

Imhotep was one of the world's earliest architects. He designed pyramids with stepped sides. After his death he was worshiped as a god.

BUILDING BLOCKS

The blocks of stone used to build the pyramids are enormous. On average, they are as big as, and weigh more than, a family car. It was a tremendous achievement to transport them, and lift them into place.

It was usual for a pharaoh to start arranging for his tomb to be built as soon as he came to power. Khufu's Great Pyramid took about 23 years to complete. Considering the tools and equipment the Egyptians had to work with, that was remarkably quick. The pyramids were built using gangs of laborers, about 18 or 20 to each gang. The gangs had nicknames, such as Vigorous or Tough, which they sometimes scratched on the pyramid stones. About 4,000 laborers were employed to build the Great Pyramid. They were mostly villagers, conscripted by the pharaoh's officials, in the same way that other men were sent to join the army. They were paid their wages in food—bread, dried meat, and beer—and lived in specially built villages set up around the construction site.

▶ The *true* pyramid

This pyramid built by Pharaoh Khafre (2520–2494 BC) is considered the *true* or perfect architectural design for pyramids. The Sphinx, half human and half lion, lies on guard.

▲ Gateway to the tombs

This impressive gateway guards the entrance to the royal burial grounds at Saqqara

▼ A new style of tomb

The earliest pyramid in Egypt, the Step Pyramid, built around 2630 BC at Saqqara.

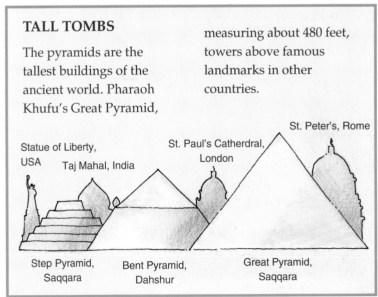

TALL TOMBS

The pyramids are the tallest buildings of the ancient world. Pharaoh Khufu's Great Pyramid, measuring about 480 feet, towers above famous landmarks in other countries.

Statue of Liberty, USA

Taj Mahal, India

St. Paul's Catherdral, London

St. Peter's, Rome

Step Pyramid, Saqqara

Bent Pyramid, Dahshur

Great Pyramid, Saqqara

prepared his tomb. His grave is probably the most famous and best-preserved of all Egyptian royal burials, but, despite its splendor and lavishness, it may not have been unique. The types of objects found there are typical of royal and noble burials. They did not only reflect Tutankhamen's status in this world, but also were all designed to help him in the world of the dead.

Buried treasures

The precious objects put into a tomb alongside a dead person were chosen with great care. They included food and drink, models of servants and guards, and even means of travel. This was because the purpose of an Egyptian burial was to help the dead person live again "for millions and millions of years." Life on earth was uncertain and sometimes sad; true happiness was to be found after death. The Egyptians believed that by

▲ **Guardian of the tomb**
The face of one of two life-size guardians of Tutankhamen's tomb. He is made of wood varnished black with his features and clothing gilded.

▶ **Death mask**
The face of Tutankhamen's mummy was covered with this funeral mask, made of pure gold, decorated with precious stones and colored glass.

▲ **Goddess protector**
The goddess Hathor, in the shape of a mother cow, watched over the body of the dead king. She wears the Sun Disk between her horns.

carefully preserving a dead body (you can see how this was done on pages 48–49), you would also preserve its spirit, and give it everlasting life.

Houses of eternity

A tomb was, therefore, a house of eternity. Often, important people designed their own tombs while they were still alive. Tutankhamen did not do this, probably because he died so young. For him, royal officials provided everything his spirit might need for its everlasting life, from food and drink to musical instruments and fans. But this new life was not lived in the tomb itself. That was simply where the body was kept. Tutankhamen's spirit, like everyone else's, had to travel to another world—the peaceful kingdom of the dead. And so the officials included all that his spirit needed for this last, dangerous journey—boats, guardian statues, clothes, and weapons.

▲ Traveling to the next world
Egyptians believed that the souls of the dead were carried to the next world on funeral boats. This boat was found in the pyramid at Giza. It was designed to take Khufu's soul on its dangerous final journey.

▼ Gilded decoration
Decoration from one of Tutankhamen's coffins. It shows the gods and goddesses who, the Egyptians hoped, would protect Tutankhamen's soul in the world of the dead.

◄ War victor
One side of a painted chest found in Tutankhamen's tomb. The sphinxes represent the king as he treads his enemies underfoot.

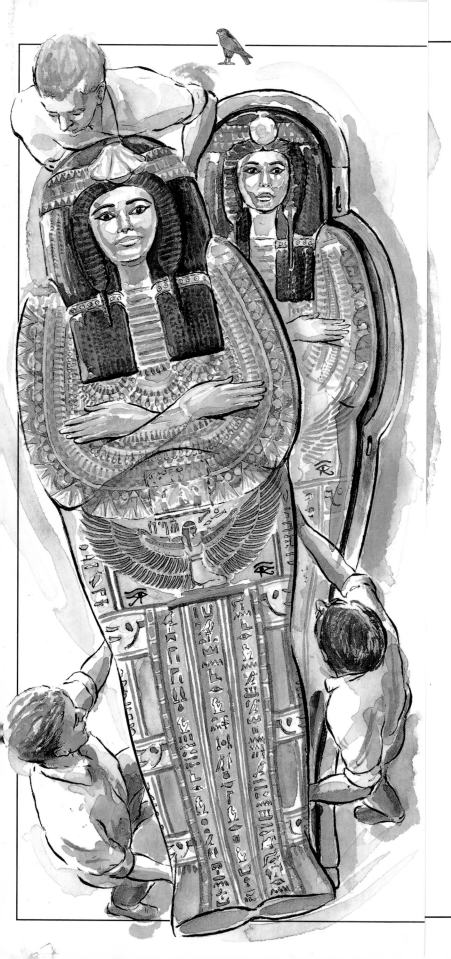

EVERLASTING LIFE

Mummies are perhaps the most famous and intriguing type of evidence to have survived from Egyptian times. It is an extraordinary feeling to be able to look at the face—however crumbling or shriveled—of somebody who lived over 4,000 years ago.

The outer casings of a mummy, and the coffin or sarcophagus in which it was buried, can tell us about the Egyptians' religious beliefs, and, sometimes, about the long, complicated funeral ceremonies they arranged. We can discover how old the mummified persons were when they died, some of the illnesses they had suffered from, and, probably, how wealthy they had been. We may even be able to find out what individual Egyptians looked like, or more accurately, how they wished to be remembered for evermore.

◀ Lifting the lid
Mummies often had more than one coffin; for example, Tutankhamen had four. They were made from wood, which was then heavily decorated on the outside with both paint and gold leaf.

▶ Canopic jars
These were used to store the liver, lungs, stomach, and intestines of the dead body. Each was mixed with scented gum, and sealed in a separate jar. Hawk-headed jars held intestines.

Making mummies was a skilled and unpleasant process. Bodies rotted quickly in the hot Egyptian sun. Many ordinary people could not afford a beautifully decorated mummy or coffin; their bodies were preserved as quickly and cheaply as possible. In contrast, the families of important people lavished a great deal of money and time in preparing the best possible mummy of their dead relative.

Preserving the spirit

The Egyptians mummified dead people in the hope of providing them with everlasting life. While their bodies survived, their spirits would also. But, in preserving their dead people as mummies, the ancient Egyptians have also helped to keep alive the memory of their magnificient civilization for many thousands of years.

▼ **Mourners and mummies**

A wall-painting showing family members weeping and saying prayers in front of a dead man. His body (which would have been mummified) is shown as it was when he was alive, to suggest that he lives on in the land of the dead.

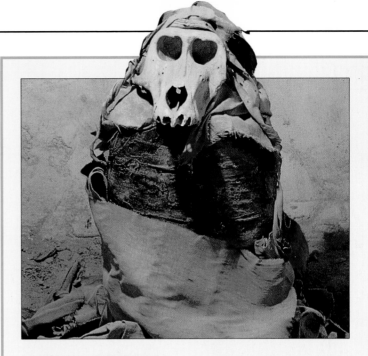

ANIMAL MUMMIES

As we have seen, the Egyptians worshiped animals kept at certain temples, like the Apis bulls at Memphis, or the cats at Bubastis, which were sacred to the goddess Bastet. To show their respect for the gods, they often turned these sacred animals into mummies when they died, and buried them close to the temple. They thought this would win them favors from the gods. Some temples even bred animals specially for sacrifice and later mummification. Thousands of dead hawks have been found at the temple dedicated to the hawk-god Horus in fields near his temple at Idfu.

▲ The remains of a mummified baboon found at the temple of Thoth, Tuna el-Gabal.

▼ Rams were considered sacred by ancient Egyptians. This mummified ram's head has been gilded and placed on a decorated board.

THE END OF THE EGYPTIAN EMPIRE

After about 1100 BC, Egyptian power began to decline. This was because of several reasons: discontent at home, enemies abroad, and the impact of new technology.

ROYAL SUICIDE

Cleopatra VII, the last independent ruler of Egypt. Her armies were defeated by Roman troops loyal to the Emperor Augustus. Cleopatra was a member of the Ptolemaic dynasty (ruling family) of Egyptian kings and queens. They had originally come from Greece, but had been settled in Egypt for around 250 years.

Cleopatra killed herself when the Romans conquered Egypt, because she preferred a noble death to foreign rule. Many centuries later, she became famous as the heroine of a play by William Shakespeare.

For many years, from about 1100–950 BC, Egypt was divided in two. Libyan merchants ruled the north, while temple priests, based in Thebes, controlled the south. Then Libyan soldiers, paid to guard the desert frontiers, rebelled. A Libyan high priest, Sheshonk, became pharaoh, and ruled successfully for many years. But more troubles followed. Around 730 BC, the Nubians invaded, and conquered land as far north as Thebes. In 663 BC, Assyrian armies attacked. They were armed with new iron weapons, and swiftly won control. A cunning Egyptian prince, Psamtik, negotiated a peace treaty, and, shortly afterwards, took over. He invited foreign merchants to come and settle in Egypt, in the hope that they would help them rebuild Egypt's wealth and power. In the short term, he succeeded, but Egypt's new prosperity made the land an even more attractive target for would-be conquerors.

CAESAR AUGUSTUS

This coin shows the head of the Roman Emperor Augustus (30 BC–AD 14), conqueror of Egypt.

Under Augustus's rule, Egypt lost its independence, but became prosperous. Trade increased, as the people of Rome were eager to buy Egyptian corn to make bread. The Roman rulers introduced new laws and heavy taxes, which the Egyptian people disliked.

Through contacts with Rome, Egyptian ideas, especially in math and medicine, together with Egyptian beliefs, spread far beyond Egypt and throughout the Roman empire.

◄ **Nubian takeover**
Nubian soldiers, from an Egyptian tomb model. They are well armed with bows and arrows.

◄ Greek mummy
Portrait mummy made for a
Greek settler in Egypt. People
often paid for portraits to be
painted showing them looking
young and well dressed. After
death, these were used to
decorate their mummies.

▼ Egypt today
Under Muslim rule, Egypt
became a rich and flourishing
state in the Middle Ages. This is
the great city of Cairo. In the
distance you can see the citadel
(fortress) topped by a graceful
mosque.

Persians, Greeks, and Romans

Invaders came again in 525 BC. Persian troops
attacked and established a new ruling family,
which governed for almost 200 years. They were
overthrown by the armies of Alexander the Great,
a brilliantly successful war leader from Macedon
in northern Greece, in 332 BC. When he died, it
was arranged for a Greek ruling dynasty, the
Ptolemies, to succeed him.

The end of independent Egyptian civilization
finally came in 30 BC, when Cleopatra, last
Ptolemaic ruler of Egypt, committed suicide, rather
than be taken prisoner by Roman troops. Not long
afterward, Egypt was declared to be a province
(colony) of Rome. In 634 AD, the remains of Roman
control were swept away, and Egypt became part of
a mighty, new Muslim empire, based in Damascus
and, later, Baghdad. The Egyptians did not fully
regain their independence until 1952.

EGYPTIAN TIME CHART

This time chart follows the progress of the Egyptian empire from its beginnings, through to its conquest by the Romans. During this time, government, architecture, religion, and scientific knowledge developed and changed.

Historians have divided Egyptian history into separate periods and these are marked according to their dates on the chart below.

EGYPT AND NEIGHBORS

The Egyptians were not the only great civilization in the Middle East. In this chart, you can see the names of Egypt's neighbors, and the times when they were powerful.

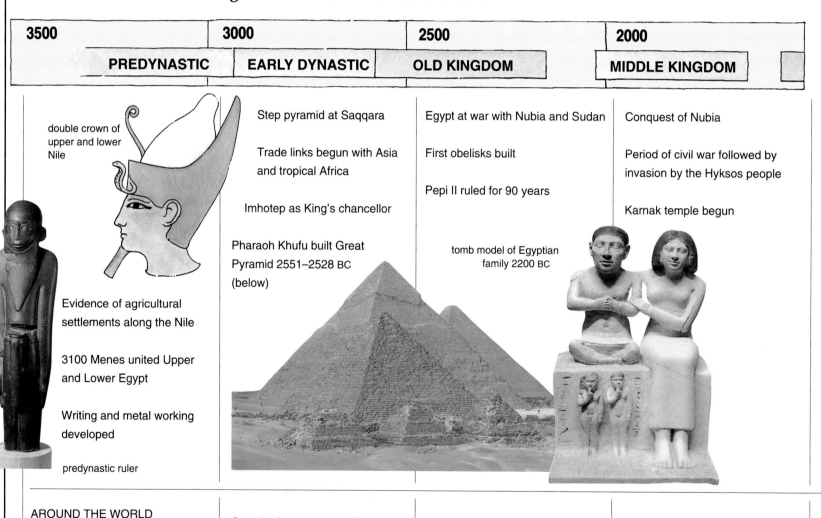

3500	3000	2500	2000
PREDYNASTIC	**EARLY DYNASTIC**	**OLD KINGDOM**	**MIDDLE KINGDOM**

double crown of upper and lower Nile

Step pyramid at Saqqara

Trade links begun with Asia and tropical Africa

Imhotep as King's chancellor

Pharaoh Khufu built Great Pyramid 2551–2528 BC (below)

Egypt at war with Nubia and Sudan

First obelisks built

Pepi II ruled for 90 years

tomb model of Egyptian family 2200 BC

Conquest of Nubia

Period of civil war followed by invasion by the Hyksos people

Karnak temple begun

Evidence of agricultural settlements along the Nile

3100 Menes united Upper and Lower Egypt

Writing and metal working developed

predynastic ruler

AROUND THE WORLD

Sumerians developed their form of writing

Growth of great cities in Erech

Start of the Minoan civilization on Crete

Stonehenge built in Britain

Indus Valley civilization flourished

Palace of Knossos built in Crete by Minoans

Growth of the Hittite empire in Asia

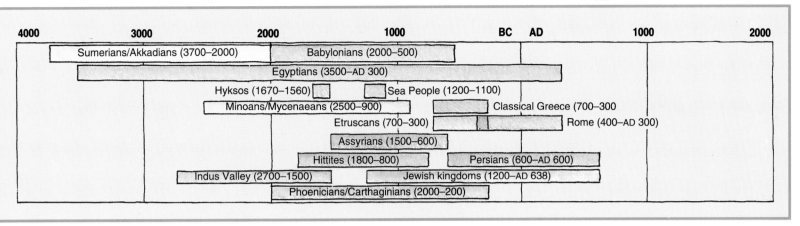

4000	3000	2000	1000	BC	AD	1000	2000

Sumerians/Akkadians (3700–2000)
Babylonians (2000–500)
Egyptians (3500–AD 300)
Hyksos (1670–1560)
Sea People (1200–1100)
Minoans/Mycenaeans (2500–900)
Classical Greece (700–300)
Etruscans (700–300)
Rome (400–AD 300)
Assyrians (1500–600)
Hittites (1800–800)
Persians (600–AD 600)
Indus Valley (2700–1500)
Jewish kingdoms (1200–AD 638)
Phoenicians/Carthaginians (2000–200)

1500	1000	500	BC	AD	500

NEW KINGDOM | | **LATE PERIOD** | **GRECO-ROMAN PERIOD** | |

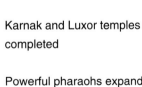

Pharaoh Akhenaton (above) built a new capital city and tried to start a new religion. After 20 years, the city was abandonded and the religion failed.

Karnak and Luxor temples completed

Powerful pharaohs expanded empire with conquests over Nubia, Syria, and Palestine

Sea peoples (probably Greeks) invaded but were driven out by Ramses II

Kingdom divided: Libyan kings in the north, priests in the south

663 BC Egypt conquered by the Assyrians

Temple at Abu Simbel built (left)

525 BC Egypt conquered by Persians

Nectanebo, the last Egyptian pharaoh

Alexander the Great from Macedon conquered Egypt

Ptolemy, the first Greek ruler of Egypt

Cleopatra, the last Greek ruler of Egypt 48–30 BC (below)

Roman Emperor Augustus died AD 14 (above)

Egypt under Roman rule until AD 395

Egyptians became Christians known as Copts

Mycenaean empire ruled in Greece

Shang dynasty established in China

Celtic people arrived in Britain

Jews established kingdom of Israel and Judah

Beginning of Olympic games

Classical Greek civilization at its height

Alexander the Great marches into India

Roman empire included most of Europe and the Middle East

Start of the Byzantine empire

GLOSSARY

(Note: Words in *italics* refer to other entries in the Glossary.)

Archaeologist Someone who studies the past by investigating the surviving remains of earlier cultures, such as buildings, burials, tools, jewels, weapons, and pottery.

Barracks A building where large numbers of soldiers live.

Bereavement The loss (usually through death) of someone who you love or care for. People who have been bereaved feel sad and sorrowful.

Cataract Massive blocks of stone in a riverbed. Cataracts are formed naturally, and there are several of them along the course of the Nile. They narrow the channel through which the river can flow, causing waterfalls, whirlpools, and strong currents. This makes it very dangerous for boats to sail nearby. In ancient Egyptian times, the First Cataract, near Aswan in southern Egypt, formed the boundary between the kingdom of Egypt and the neighboring land of Nubia.

Centralized Administered by a single strong government, based at one place in a country, rather than by several smaller, local governments.

Community The social group in which people live. Communities provide friendship, security, and help in times of trouble. In ancient Egypt, most people lived in village communities. A minority lived in towns. There, they formed neighborhood communities, and communities of merchants and craftworkers.

Conscript Someone who is forced to join the army and fight as a soldier. Also used to describe people who were forced to work for the Egyptian government in other ways—for example, by building the pyramids.

Cult A form of religious worship.

Delta The marshy area in the north of Egypt where the Nile River flows into the Mediterranean Sea. The delta lands were rich and fertile, and grew plentiful crops. They were also the home of many wild animals and birds. *Pharaohs* and other wealthy Egyptians enjoyed hunting in the delta.

Disinfectant A substance that kills bacteria. The Egyptians used oils and gums from plants as disinfectants, as well as a mineral known as *natron*, which they quarried in the desert.

Dynasty Ruling family.

Environment Surroundings, including the soils, plants, wildlife, and climate of a particular place.

Evidence Objects or documents surviving from the past that can be used by *archaeologists* and historians to tell us what life was like in vanished civilizations.

Export To sell goods abroad.

Ferment To change liquids containing sugars or starches into wine or beer by the action of yeast. The yeast feeds on the sugars and starches, and converts them into alcohol. The Egyptians allowed a mixture of old bread and water to ferment into beer.

Fertile Able to grow good crops. Soils are fertile because they contain substances that provide essential nourishment for plants to grow. These substances come from manure, rotting vegetation, and bacteria in the soil.

Flax The plant from which linen is made. Flax likes damp soils, and so it flourished beside the Nile. It grows more than three feet (1 m) tall, and has attractive blue flowers. After flowering, its stems are cut and soaked in water, until the outer casing rots away. This leaves long, strong fibers, which are spun and then woven into cloth.

Hieroglyph Picture-writing.

Innovation A new invention.

Inscription Writing or *hieroglyphs* carved on stone or, less often, on metal.

Irrigation Bringing water to dry land, to enable it to grow crops. The Egyptians dug deep irrigation channels to bring Nile waters to their fields, or they lifted water from the river using simple machines like a *shadoof*.

Laborers People who do hard physical work.

Life expectancy How long someone born into a particular civilization might expect to live, if lucky enough to escape accidents or serious illness. Life expectancy is usually measured from birth.

Ma'at The Egyptian word for "good order" or "doing what is right."

Mortuary A building where dead bodies are stored, or a temple built as a memorial after someone's death.

Mummy The preserved body of a dead person or animal.

Myrrh A sweet-smelling sticky gum, produced by plants. Used by the Egyptians as a perfume and as a *disinfectant*, to help preserve *mummies*.

Natron A substance rather like salt, which the Egyptians found in the desert and used to dry out and help preserve dead bodies being turned into *mummies*.

Nome A government district, ruled by local officials. Egypt was divided into forty-two nomes. Taxes and *conscripts* were collected separately from all the nomes.

Papyrus A reed-like plant that grew along the banks of the Nile. Its stems were pounded together to make thin sheets, which the Egyptians used like writing paper. Many books and documents written on papyrus still survive; they contain valuable evidence about ancient Egyptian civilization.

Parasite A plant or insect that lives by taking nourishment from another living creature. Some parasites, such as tropical worms, can cause serious illnesses in humans.

Petitioner Someone asking for a favor, or seeking help.

Pharaoh The Egyptian word for king. It comes from two other Egyptian words "per" (royal) and "aoh" (house).

Province District.

Quern A hand-powered machine for grinding grain. It was made of two large lumps of stone, which fitted one on top of the other. Grain was placed between the two stones, and the upper one was pushed slowly around and around. As it turned, it crushed the grain, and ground it into flour.

Regent Someone who rules on behalf of a king or queen. Often, a regent is appointed when the rightful king or queen is still a child, and is too young to run the government.

Rituals Prayers, processions, and ceremonies. The Egyptians had many rituals; some were used to worship the gods, others were used when placing a *mummy* in its *tomb*.

Scribe A highly trained person who could read and write *hieroglyphs*. The *pharaohs* employed many scribes to record their laws, to keep records of finance and *taxation*, and to send messages to local governors giving their orders. Egyptian scribes also wrote books about their religion, about the way to bury the dead, and about medicine, as well as songs, stories, and poems.

Shadoof A simple machine, made of a long pole with a bucket at one end and a weight at the other. The pole is fixed to a strong post, and is able to easily swing around. The Egyptians used shadoofs to lift water from the river and pour it on their fields.

Shift A straight, simple dress.

Shrine A holy place where the gods were worshiped.

Silt Fine particles of soil and decayed vegetation carried along by the Nile floodwaters and left behind on the fields when the floods went away.

Staple food A basic food that gives most people their nourishment.

Taxation Money collected by government from all citizens to pay for national needs, such as the army and government officials. Taxes were also used to pay for the magnificent *temples* and *tombs* constructed for the *pharaohs*.

Technology The use of tools and machines to perform essential tasks, such as building, farming the land, or weaving cloth. Ancient Egyptian technology was simple, but the Egyptians used it well to produce spectacular buildings and to support a rich civilization.

Temple A grand building where the gods are worshiped.

Tomb A place where dead bodies are buried.

Treaty An agreement made between different countries.

Tribe A group of people, often related or descended from a common ancestor, who live and work together and are loyal to one another.

Tribal Belonging to a *tribe*.

Tribute Precious goods or gold that conquered peoples were forced to pay to the Egyptian government.

Yeast A single-celled living organism, like a very simple plant.

Yield The amount of crops grown and harvested. For example, in a good year, a single apple tree might yield 100 apples. In a poor year, it might yield only 10.

INDEX

(Page numbers in *italics* refer to illustrations and captions.)